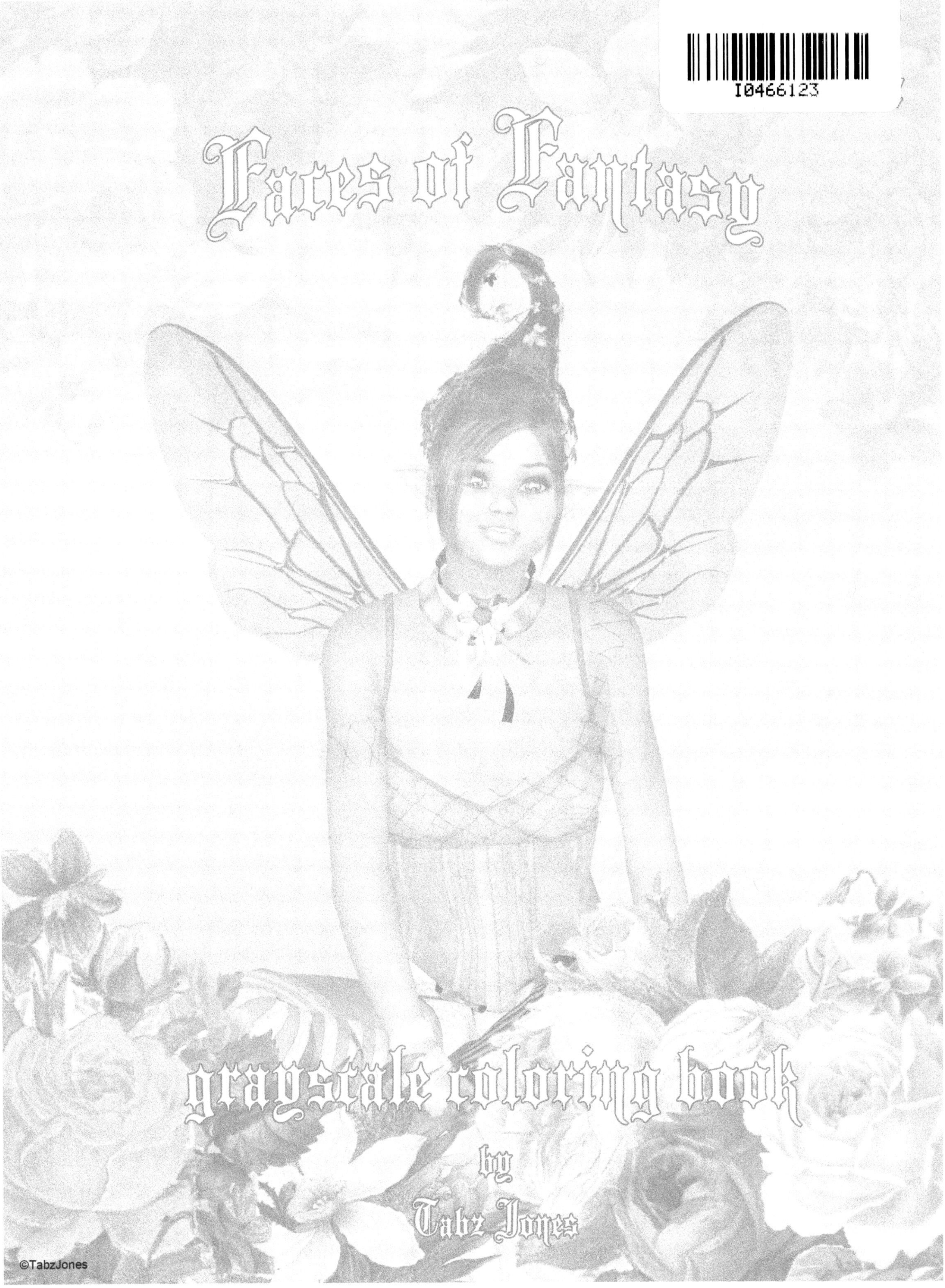
Faces of Fantasy
grayscale coloring book
by
Tabz Jones
©TabzJones

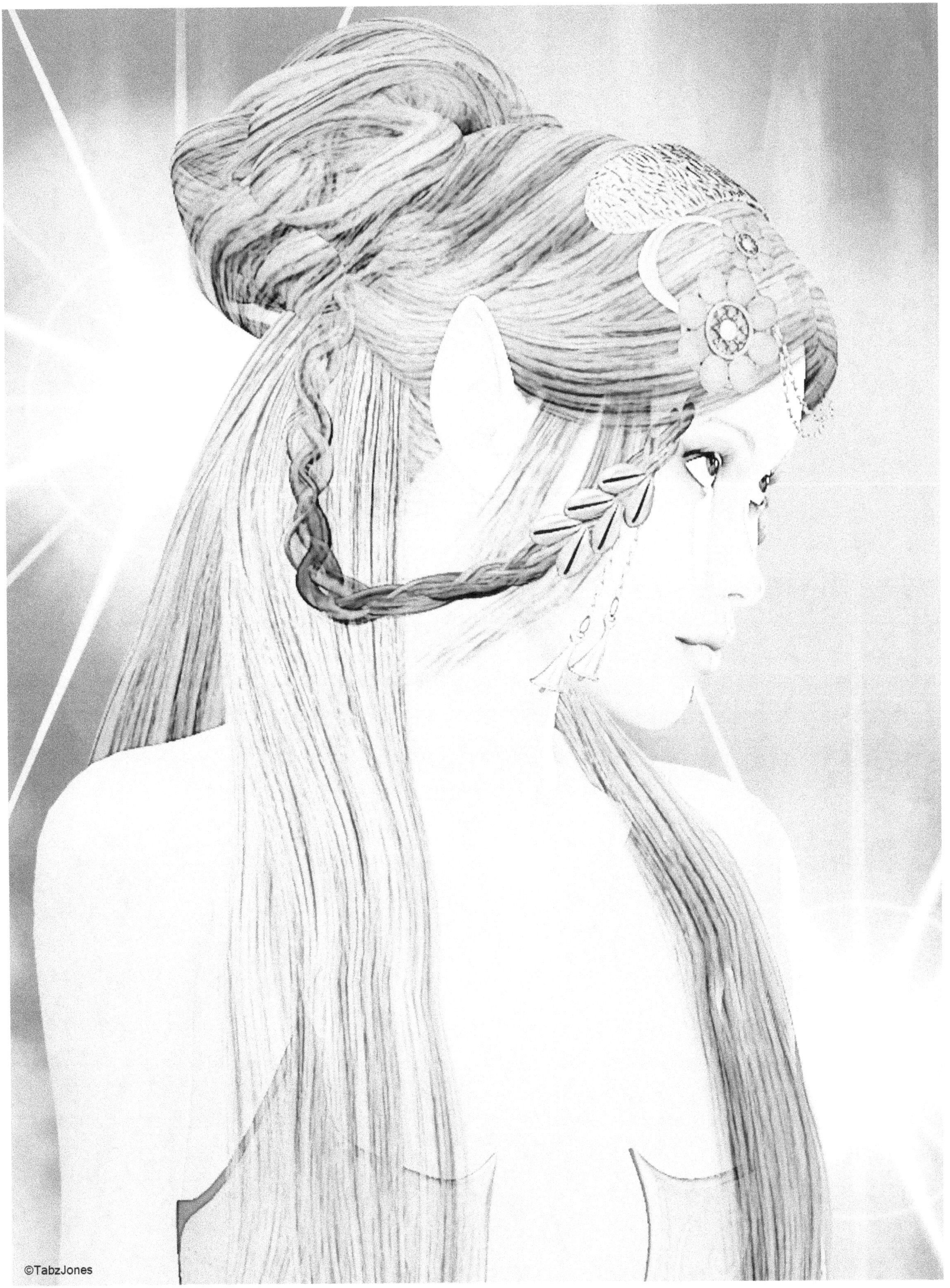

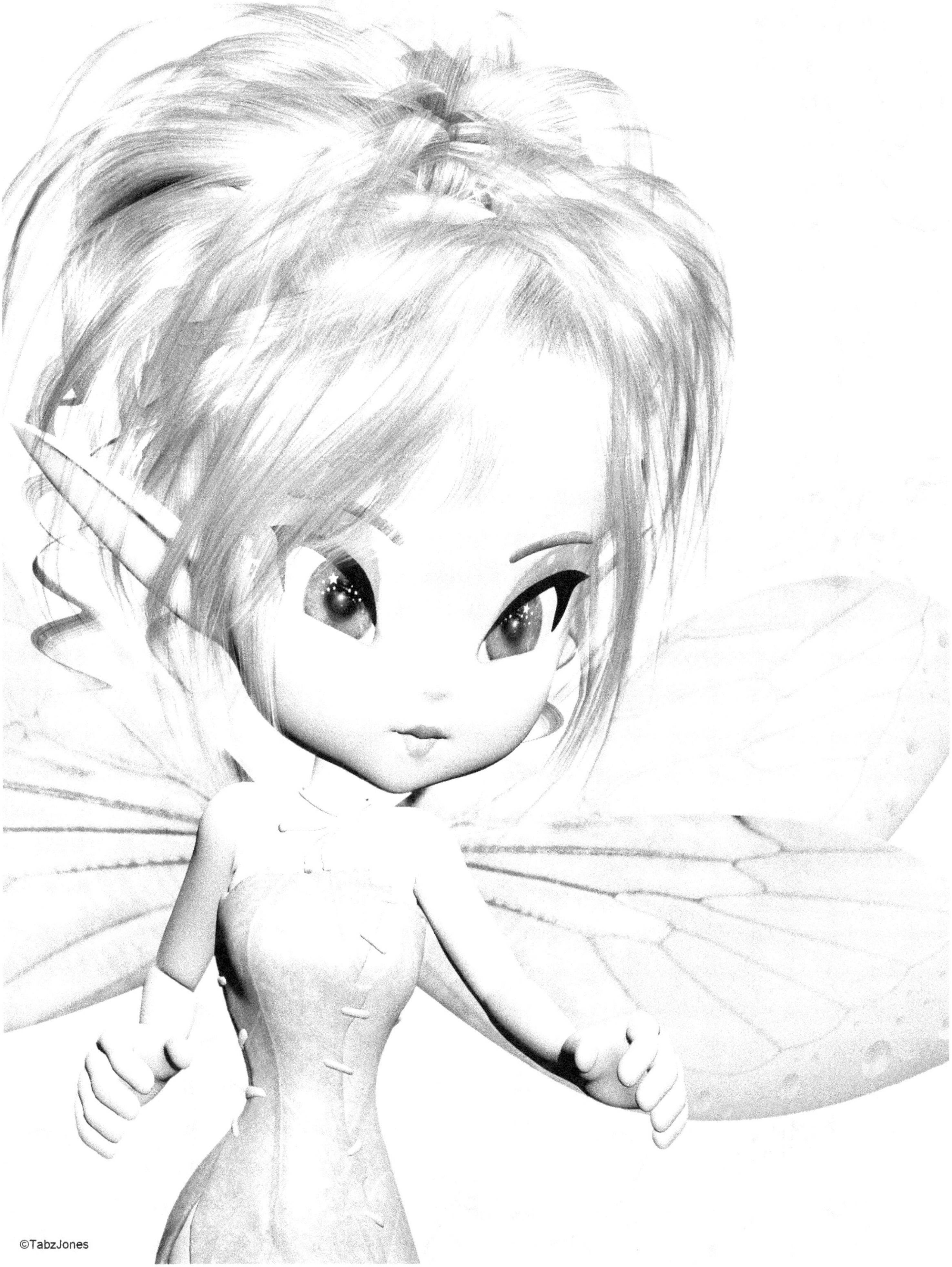

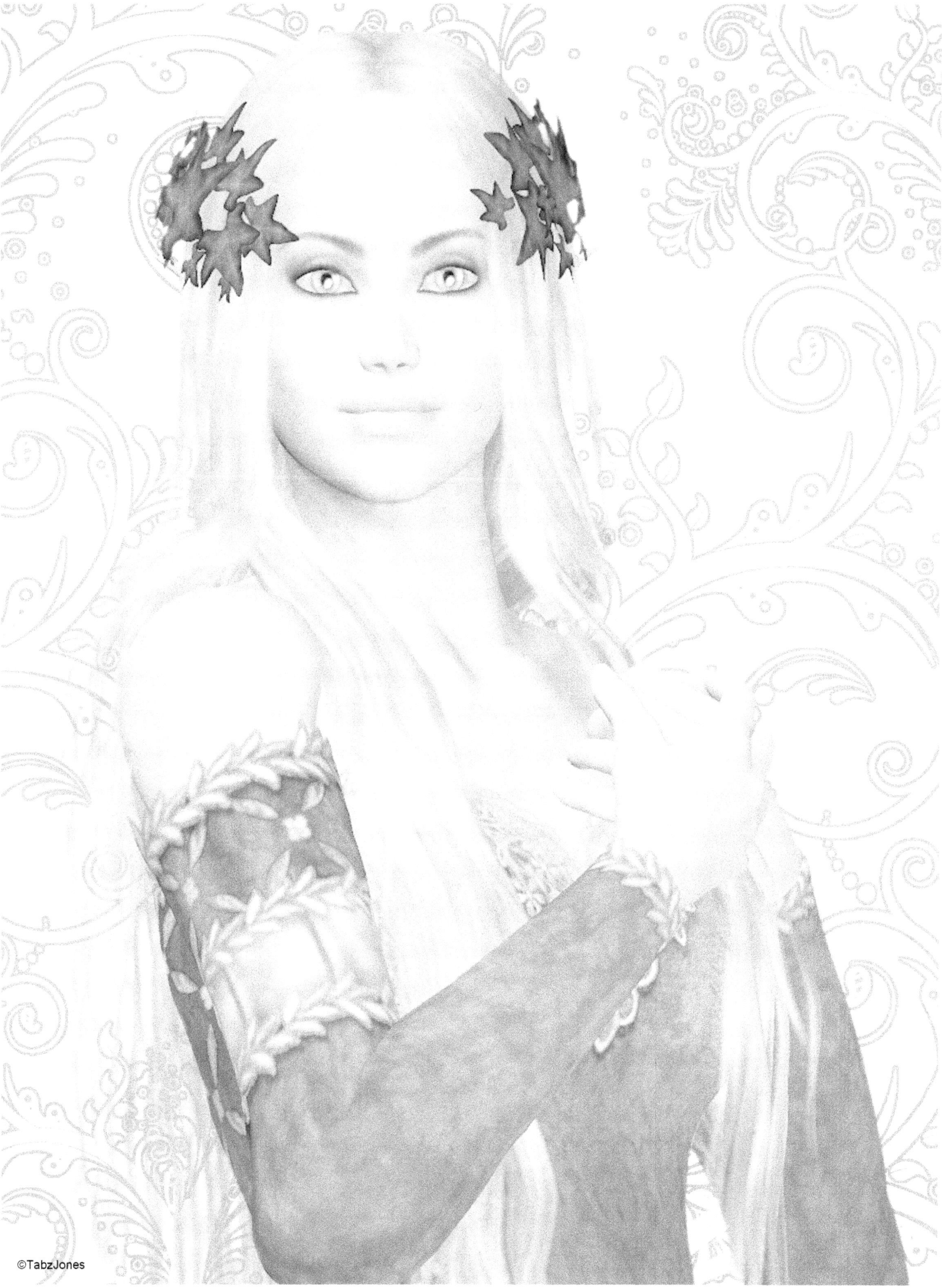

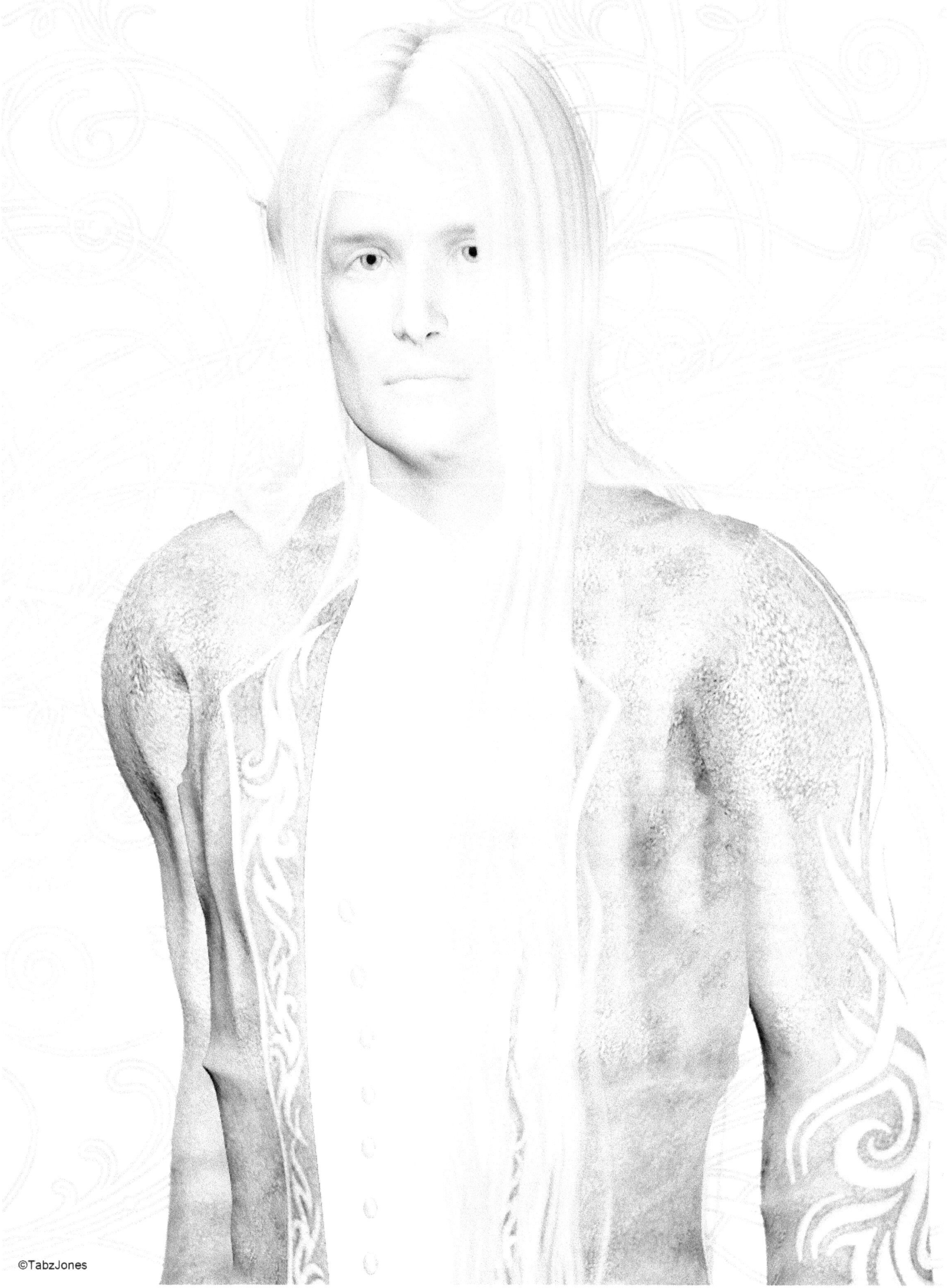

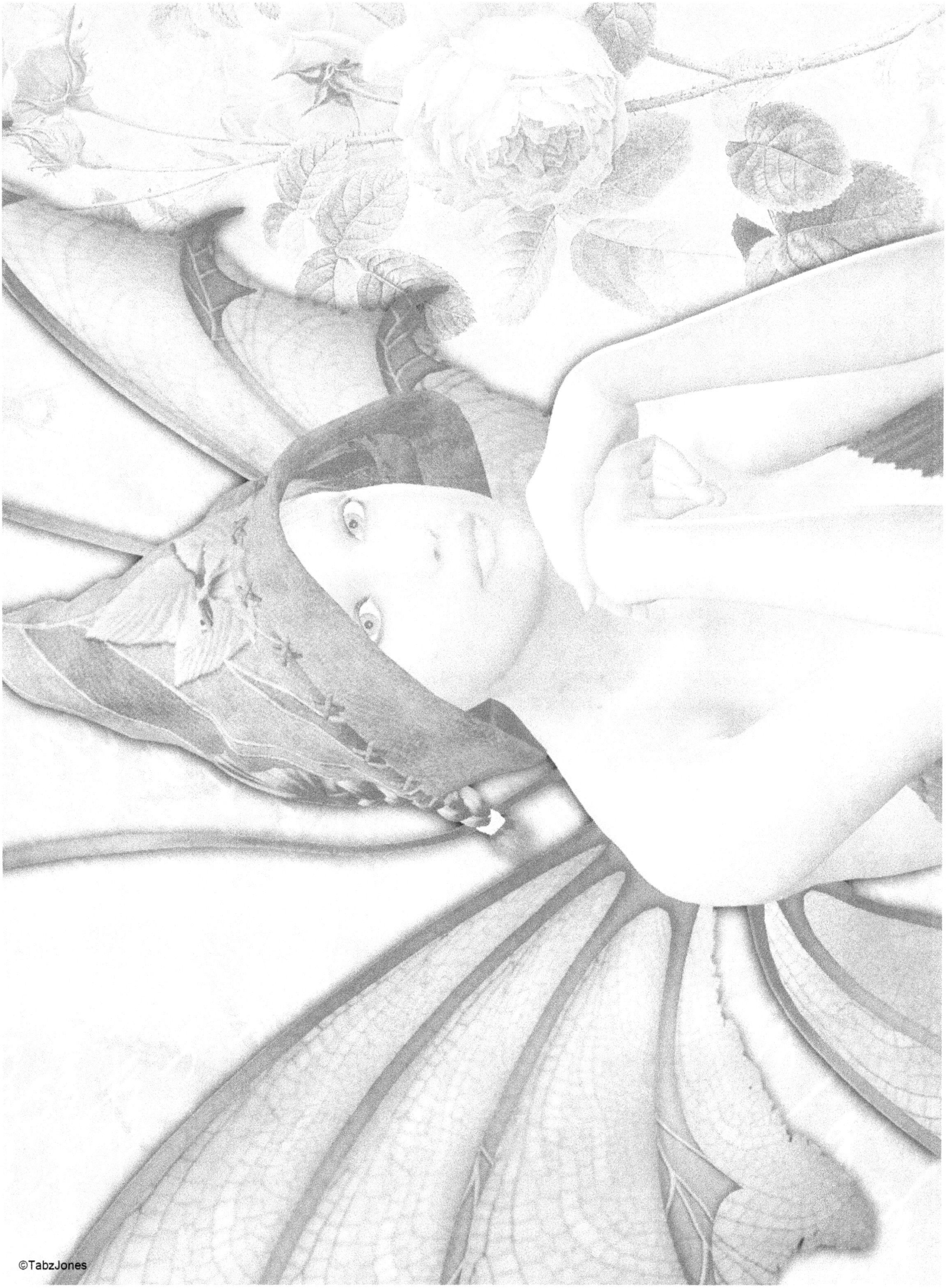

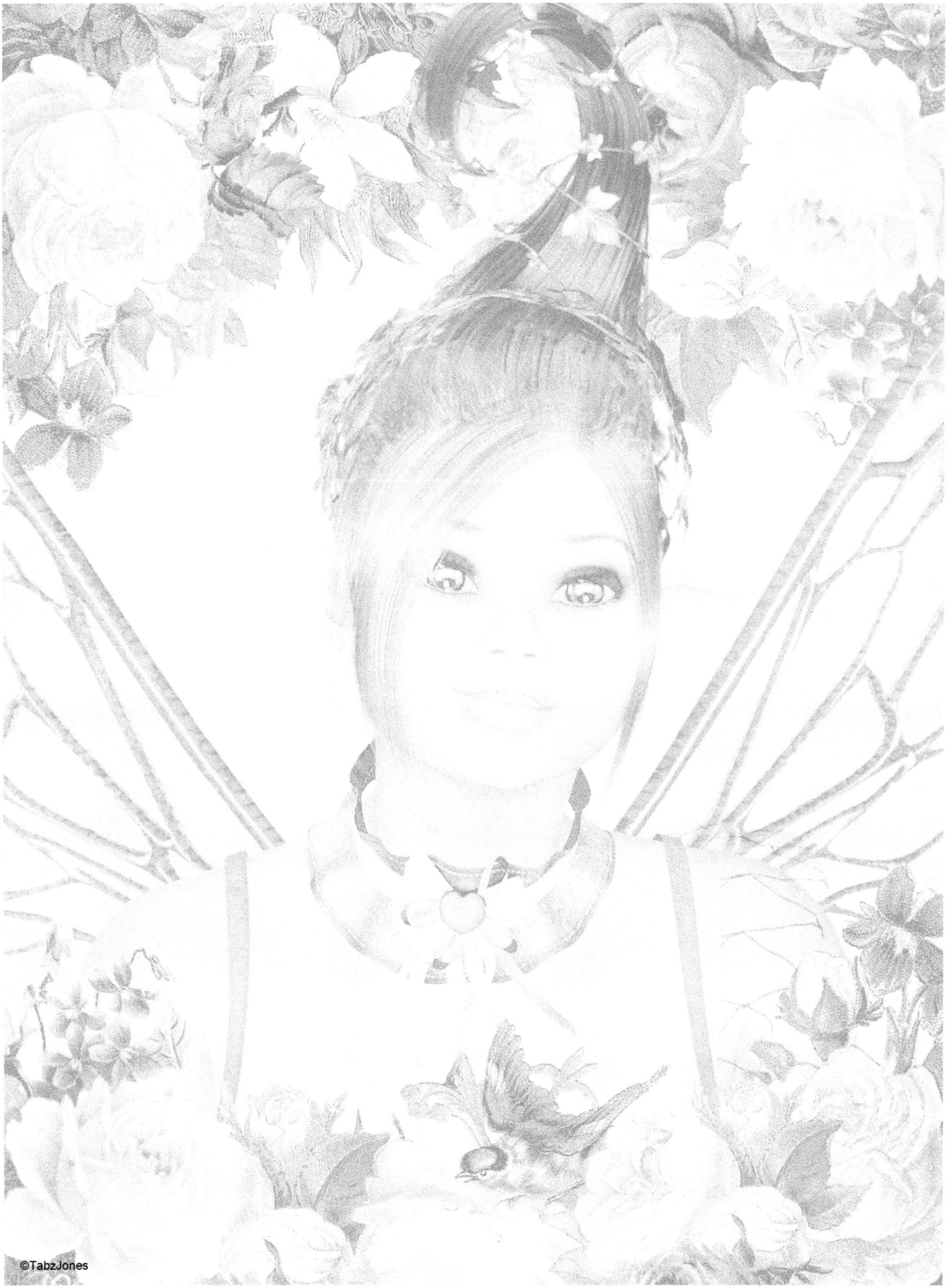
©TabzJones

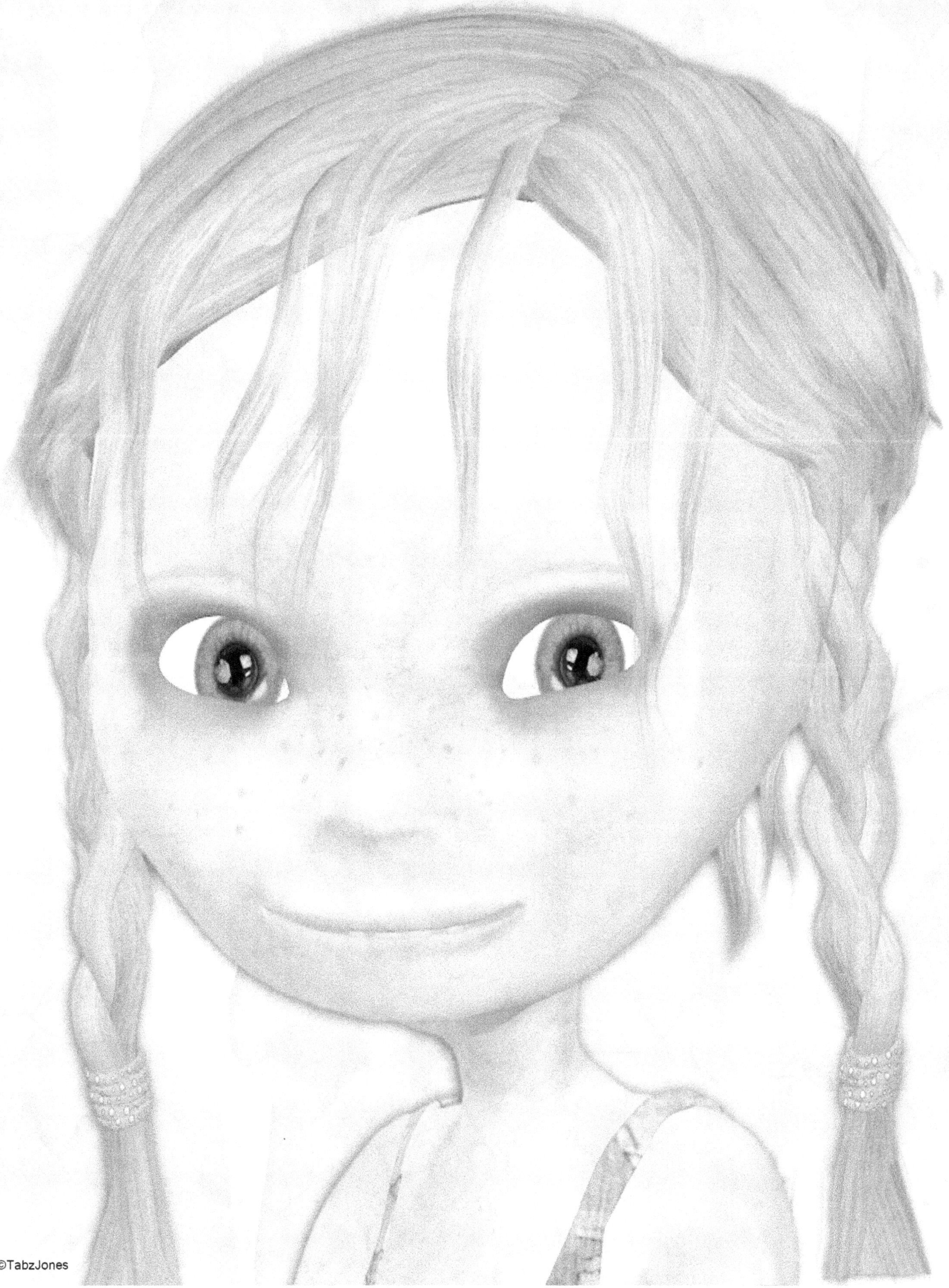

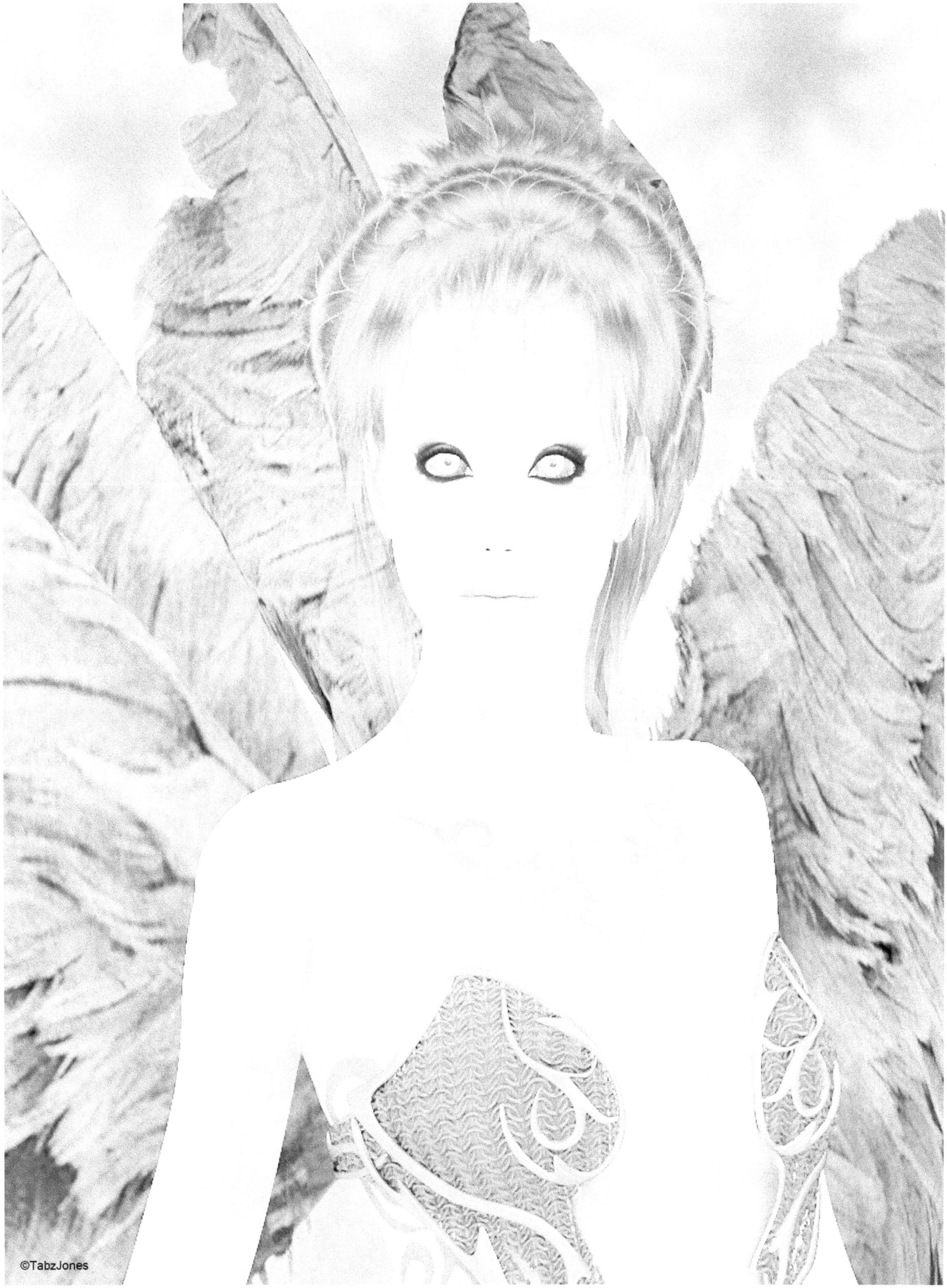

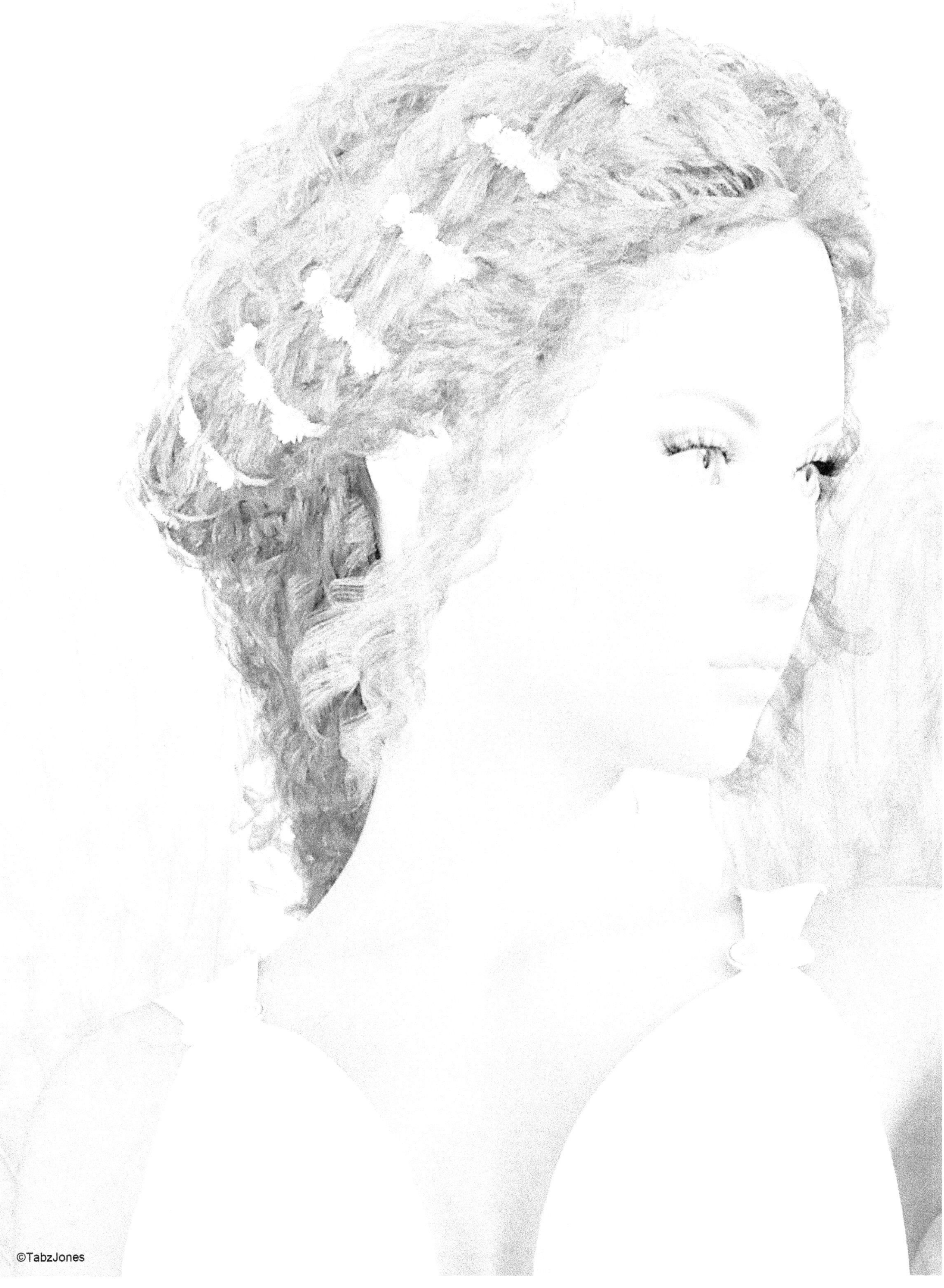

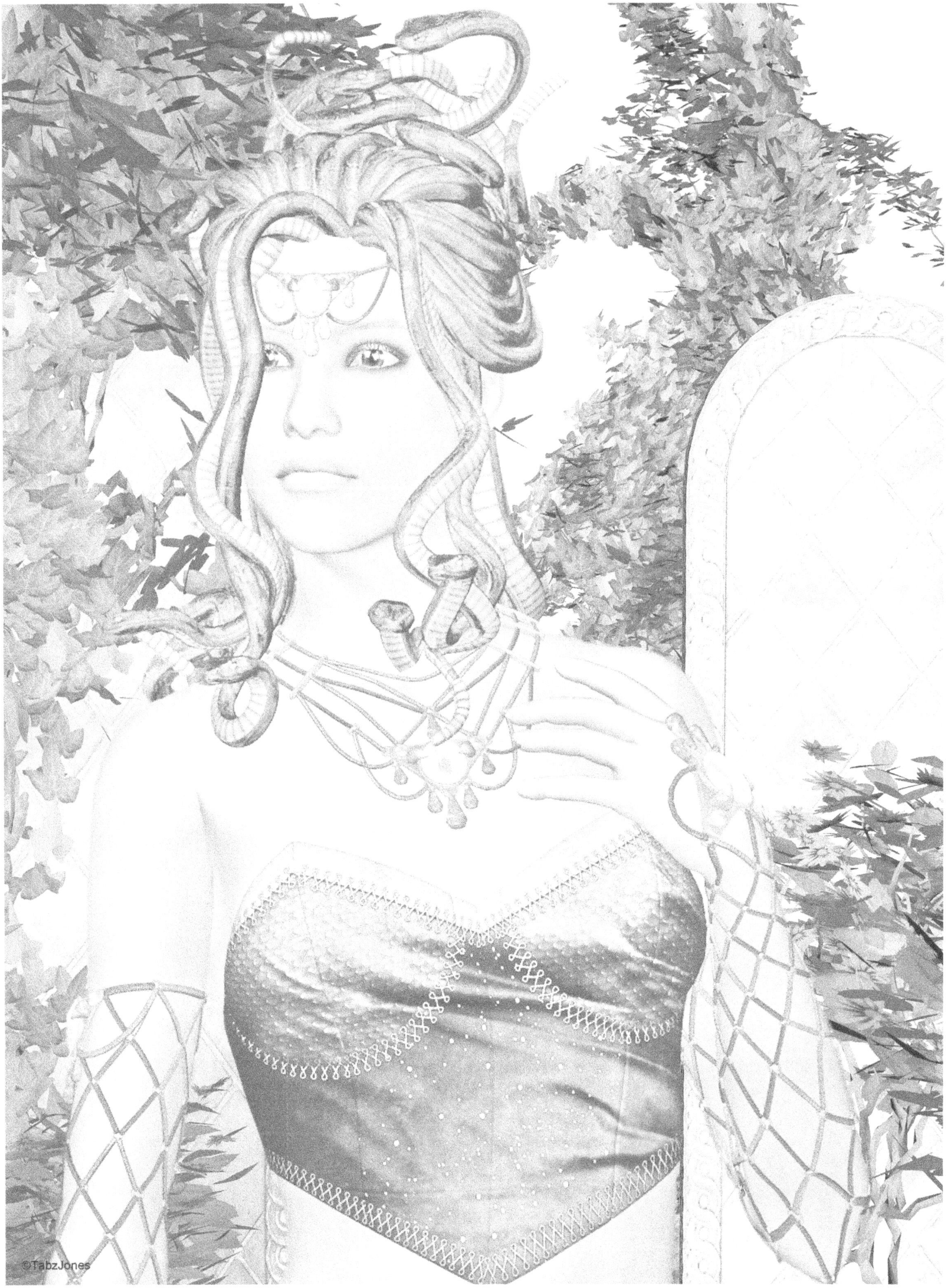

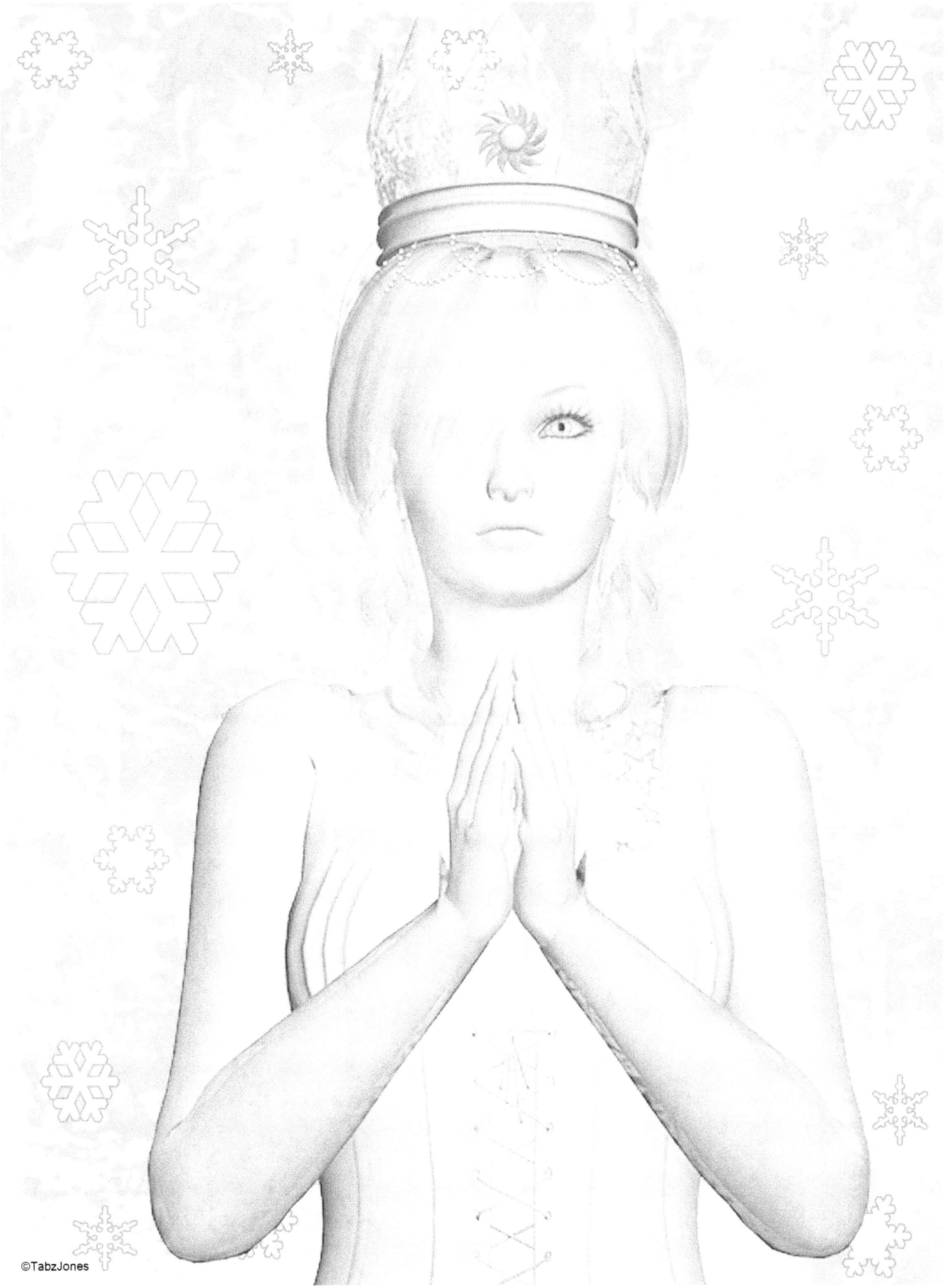

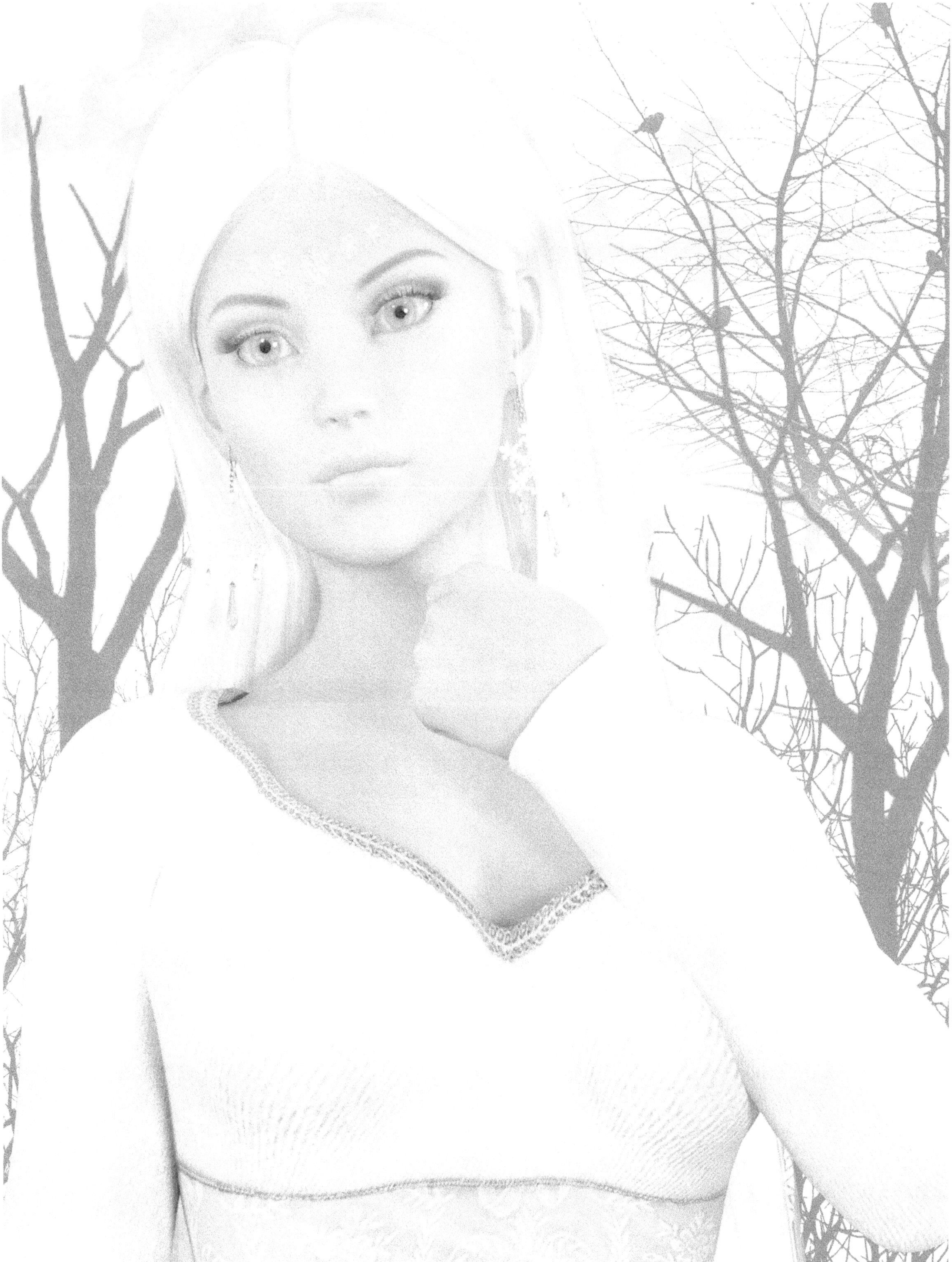

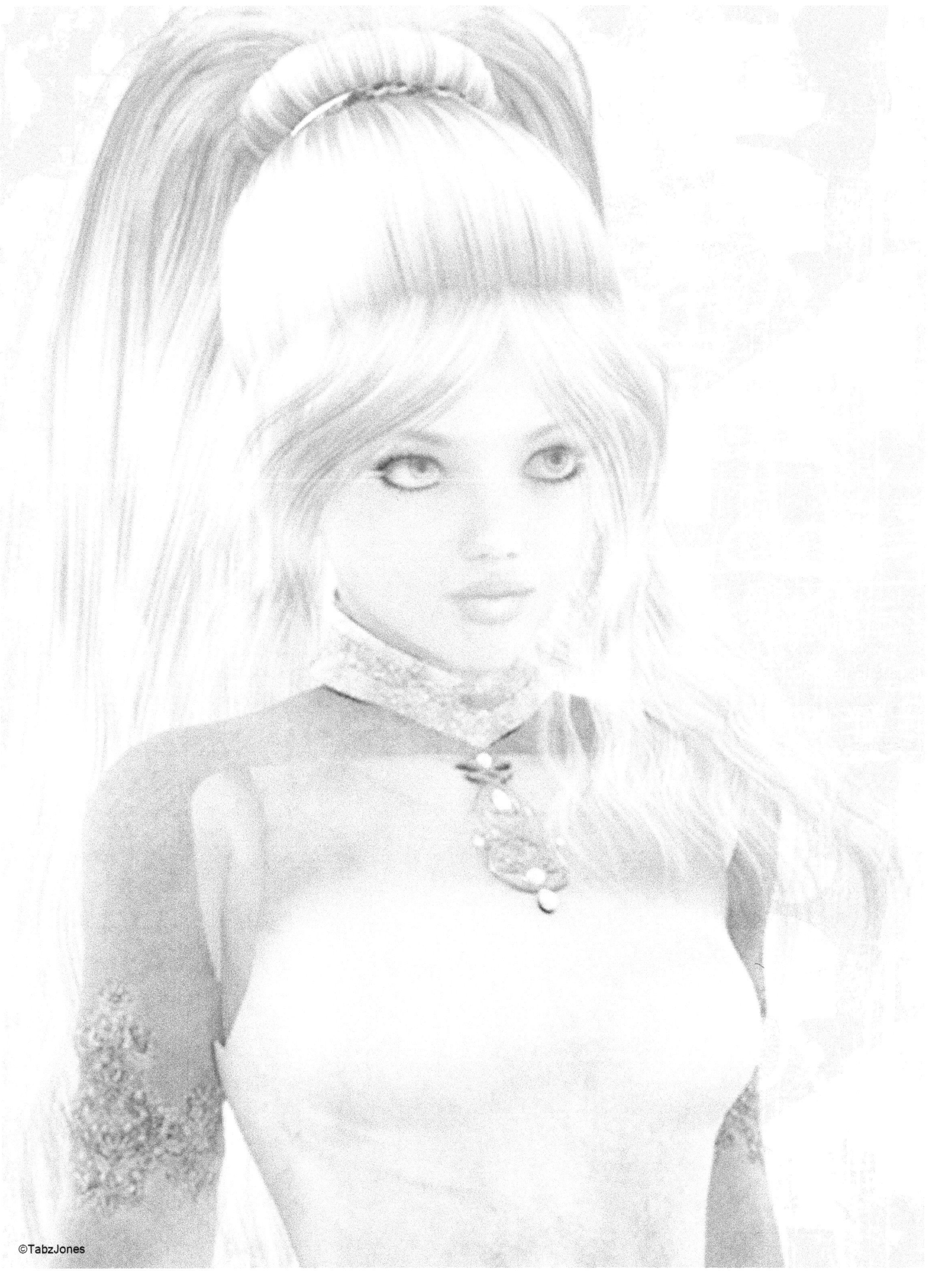

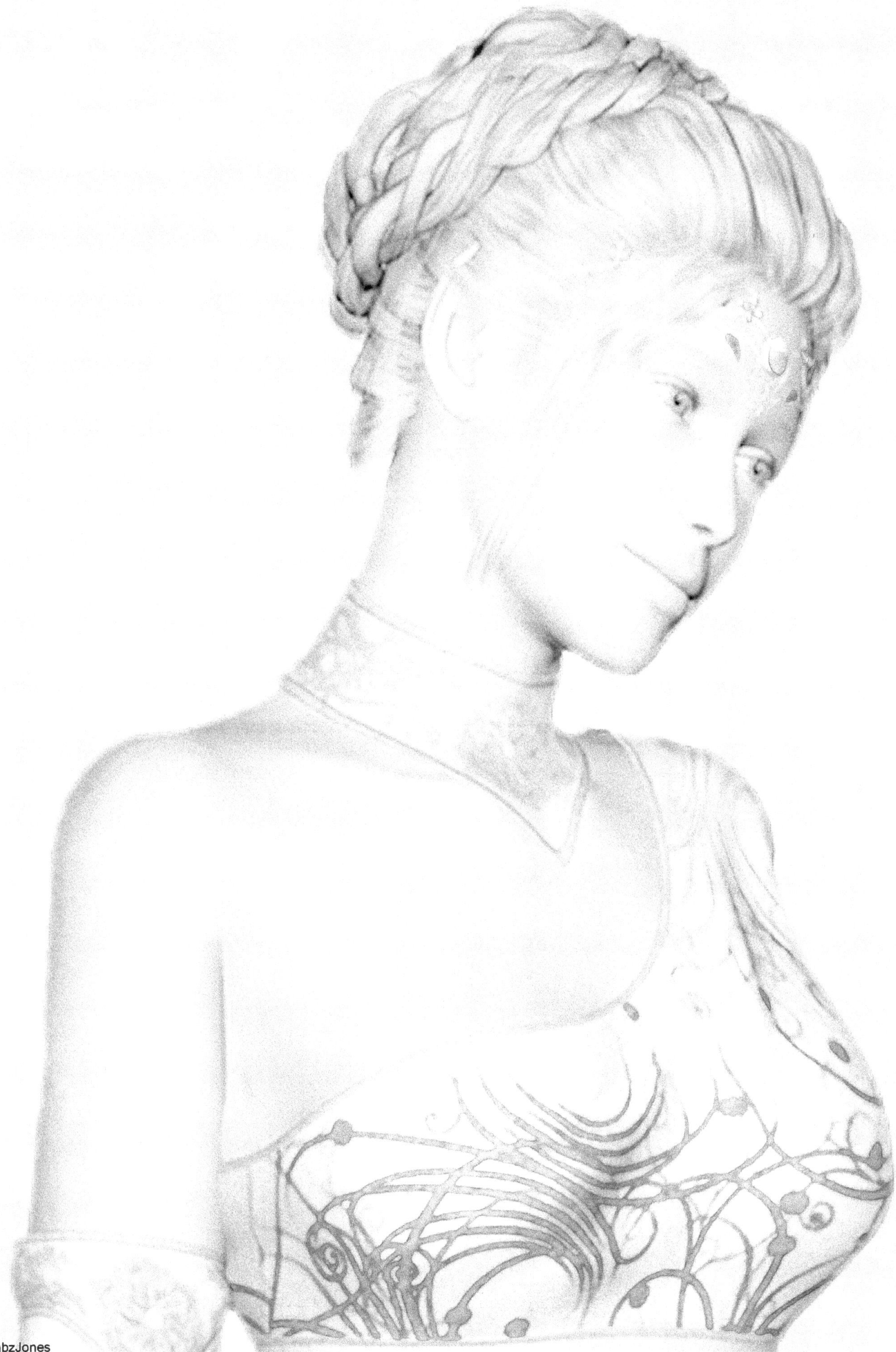

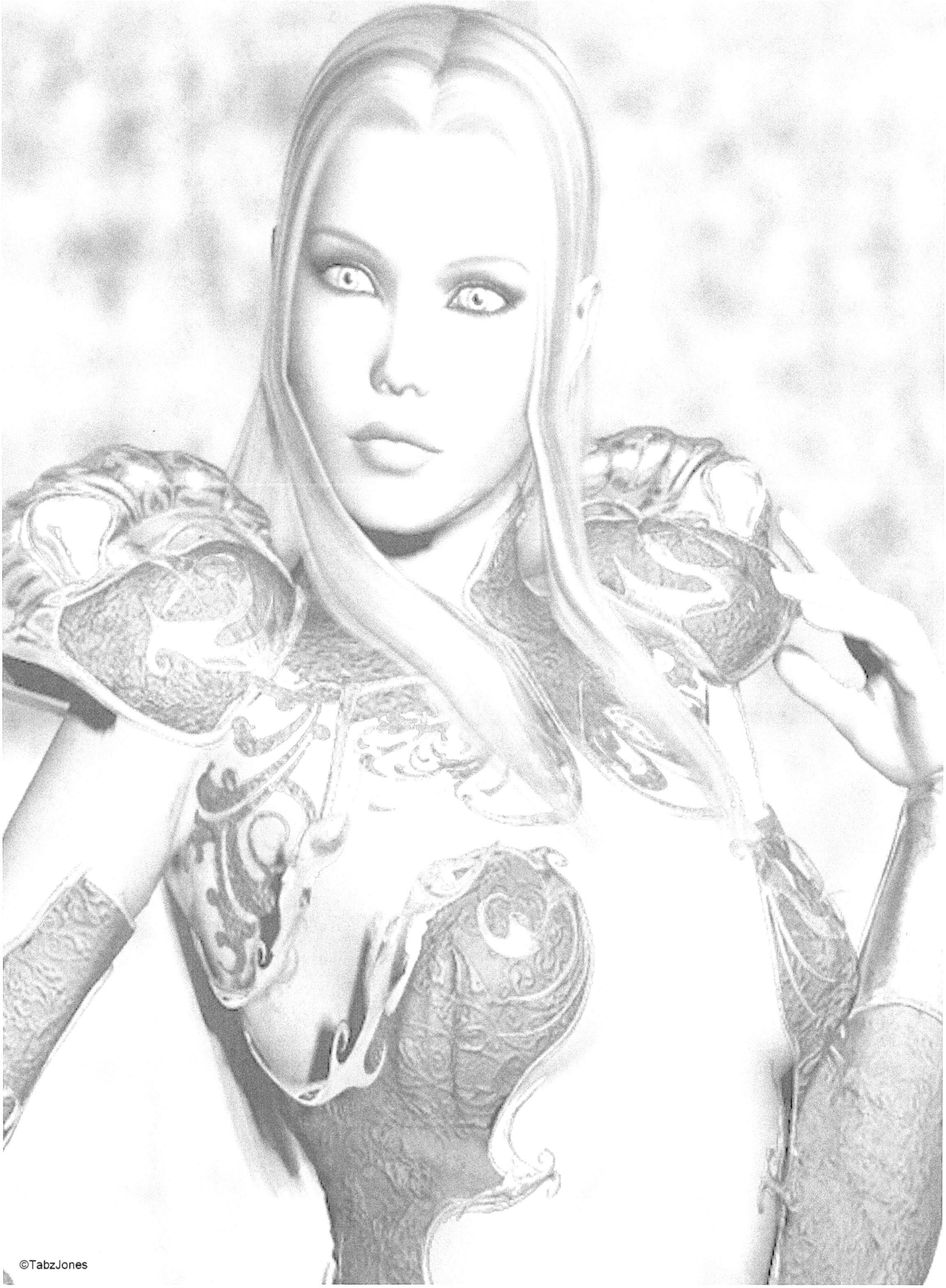

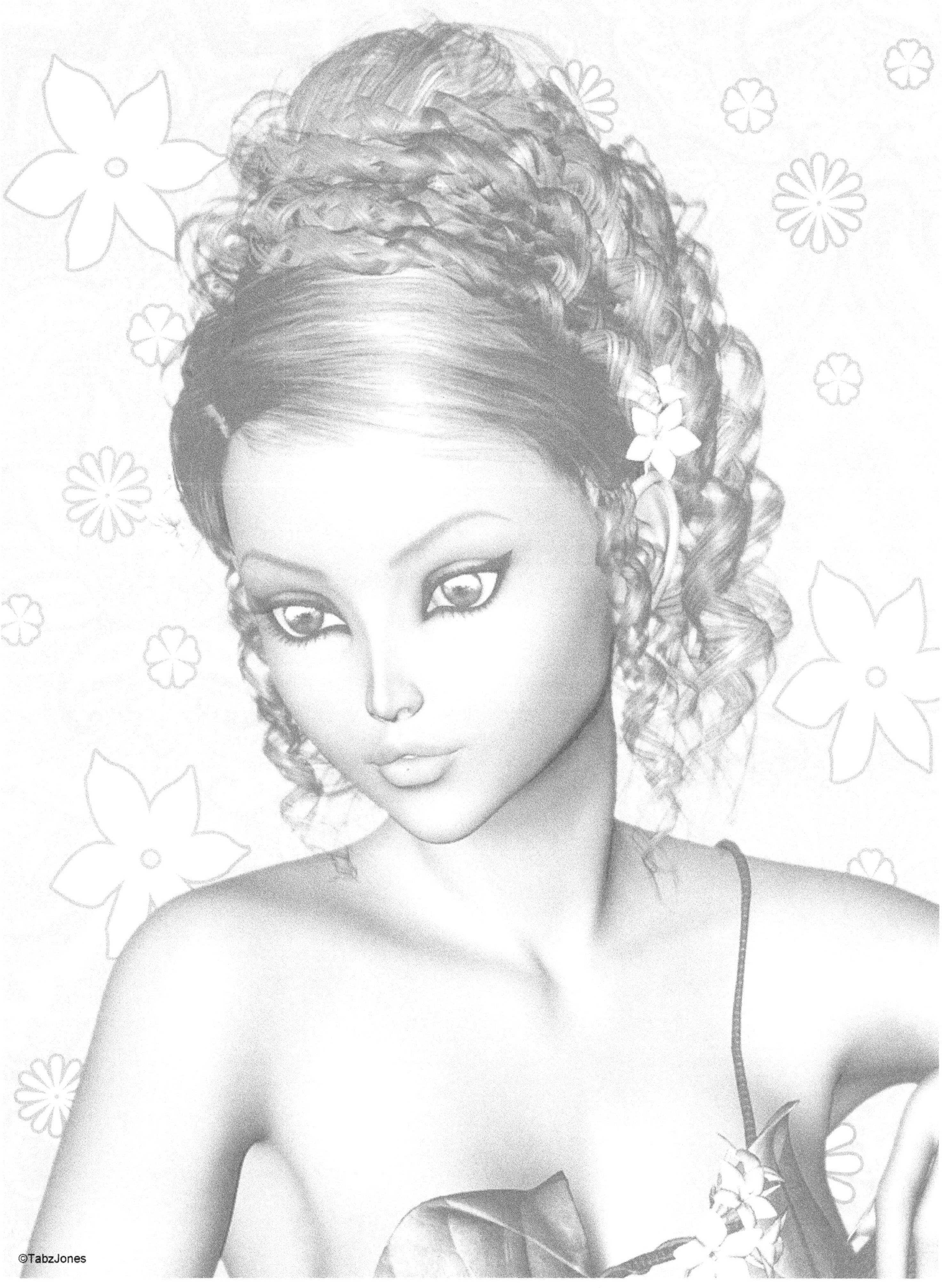

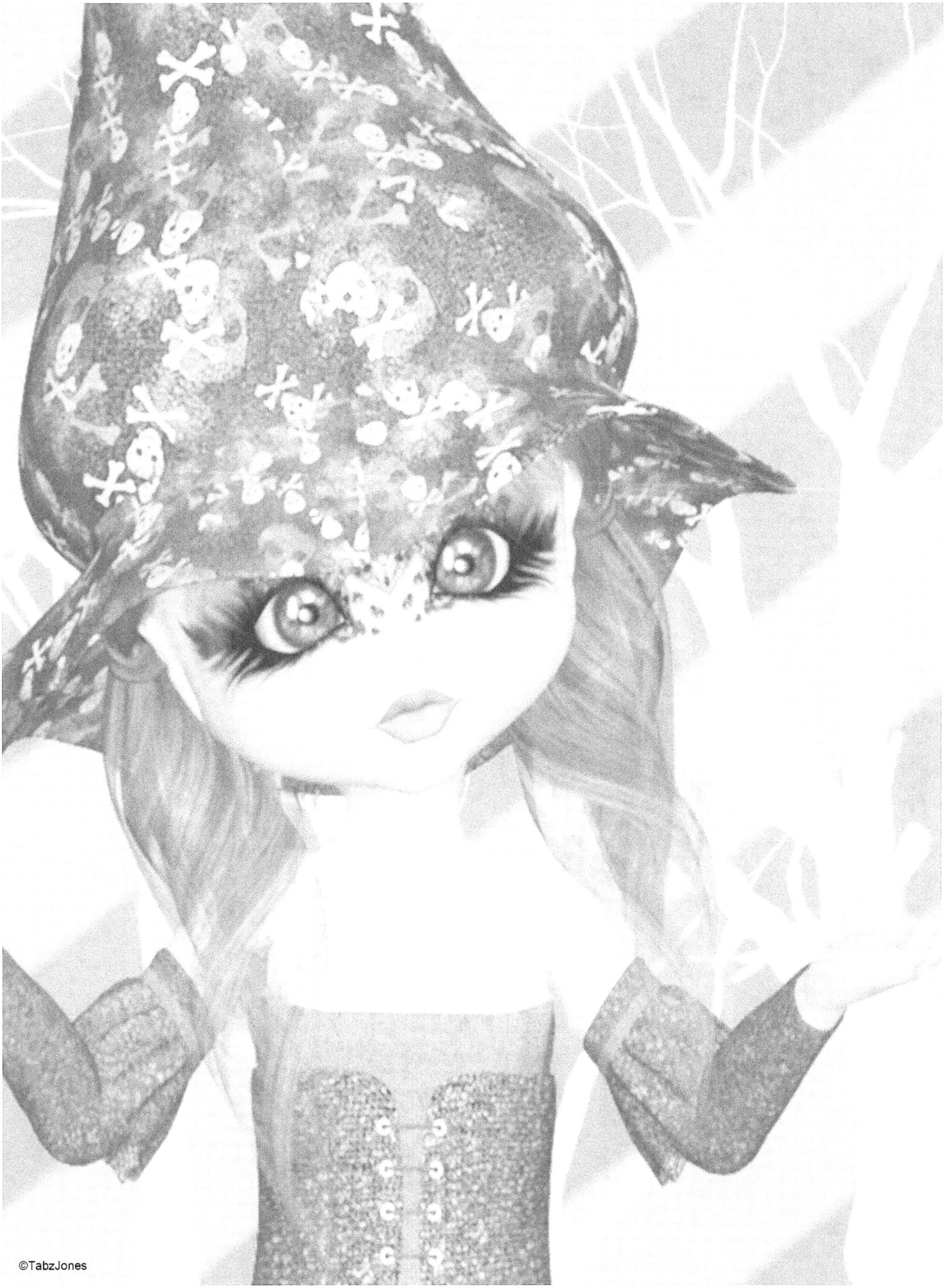

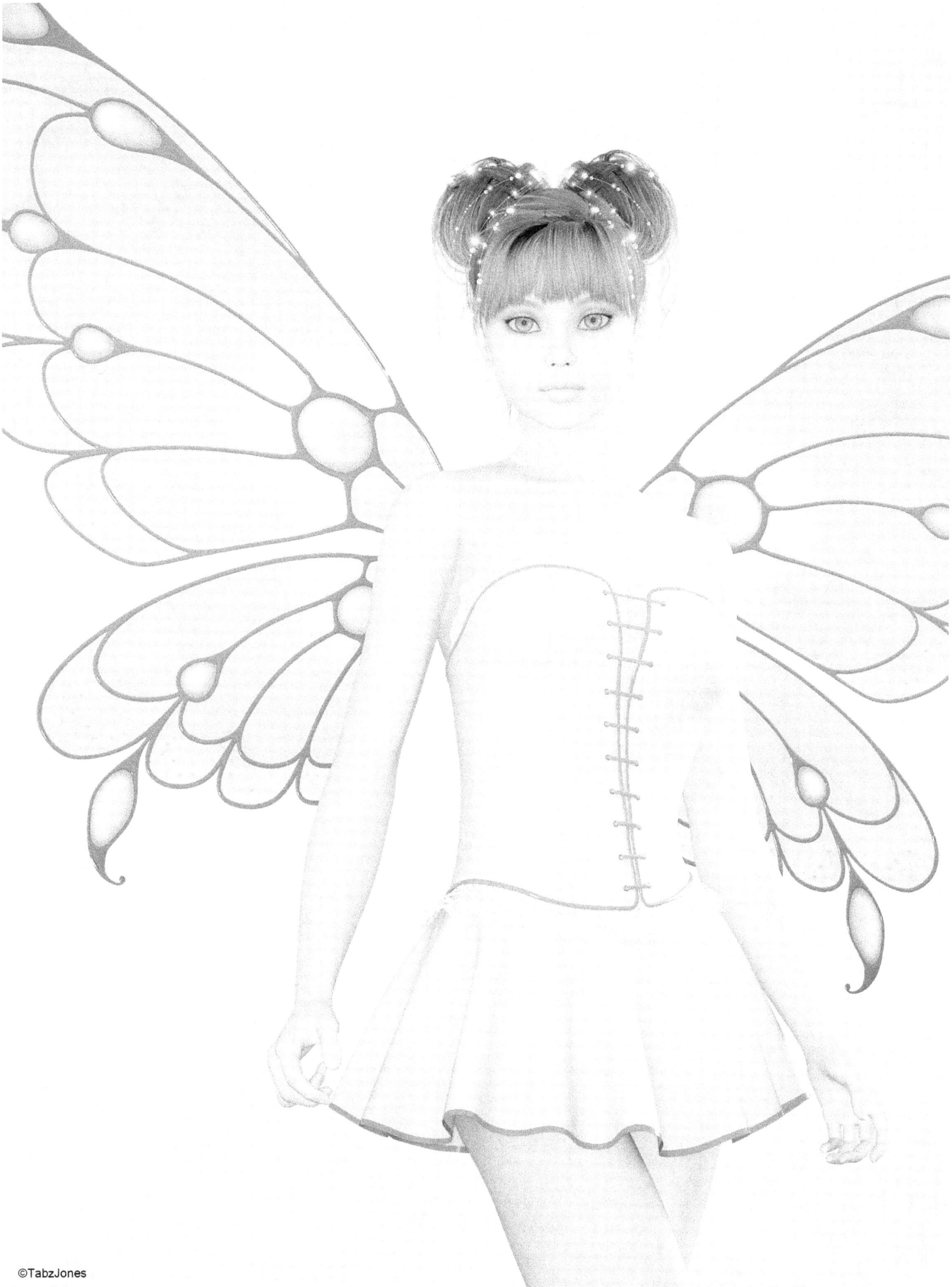

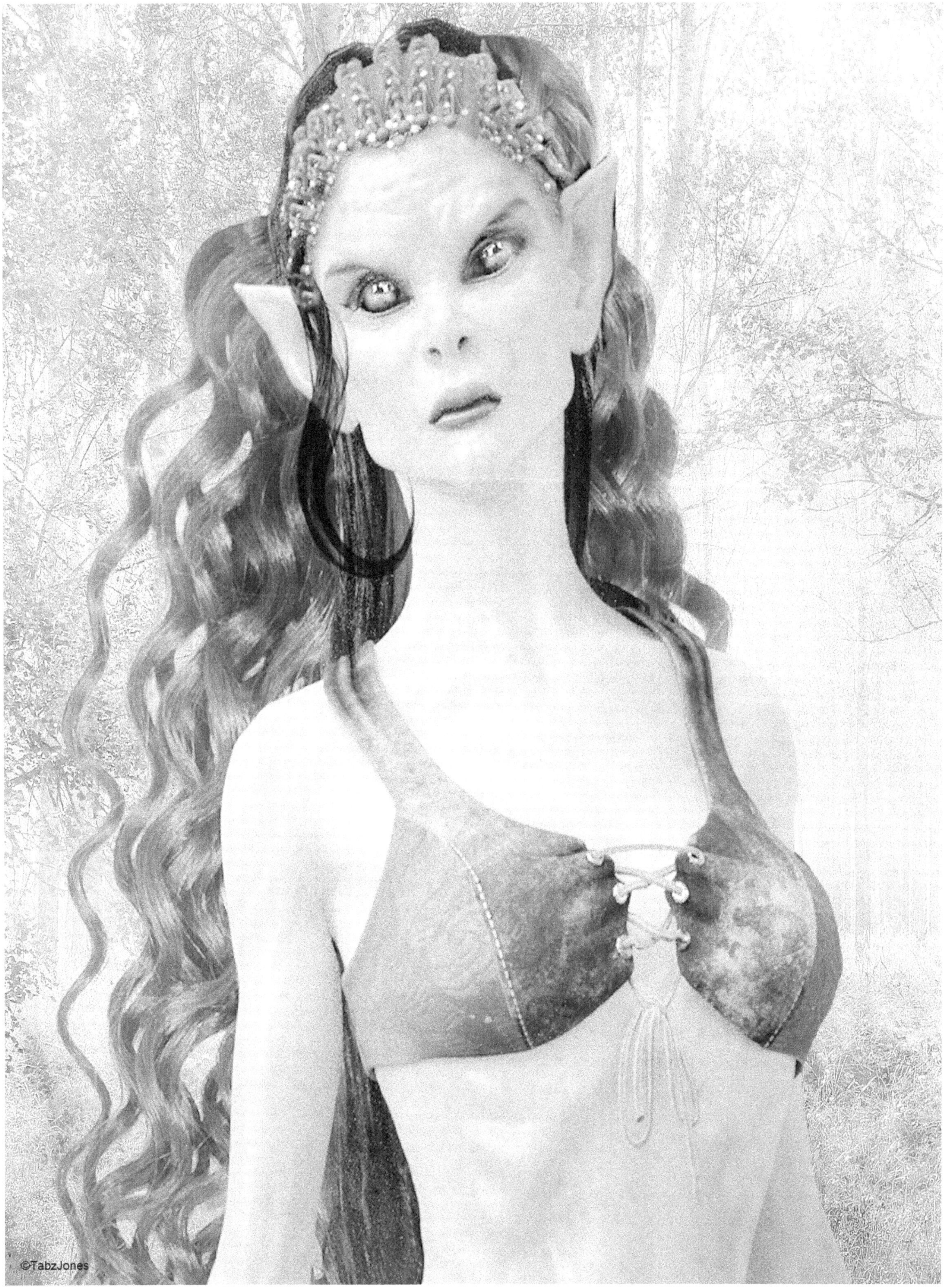
©TabzJones

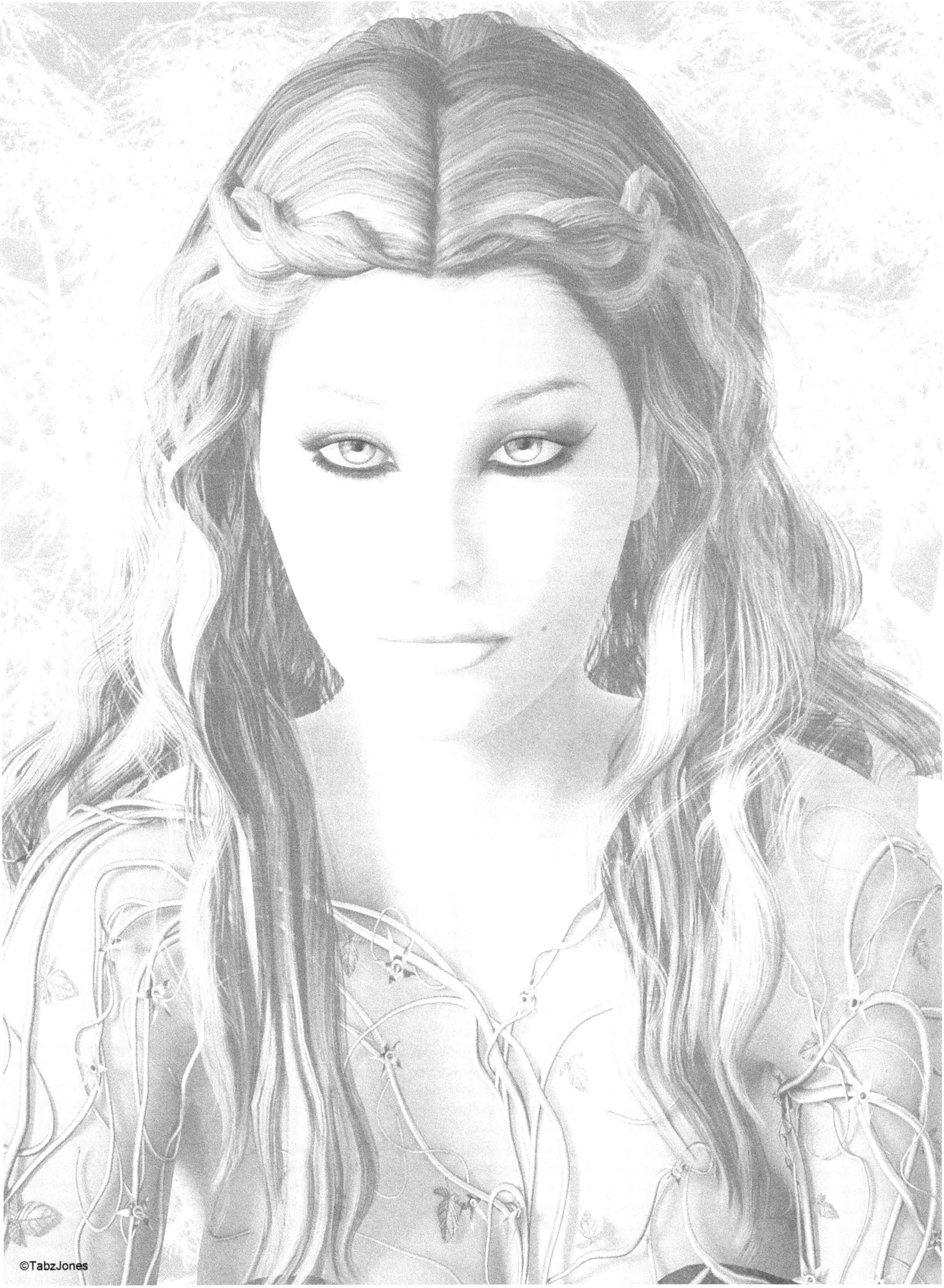

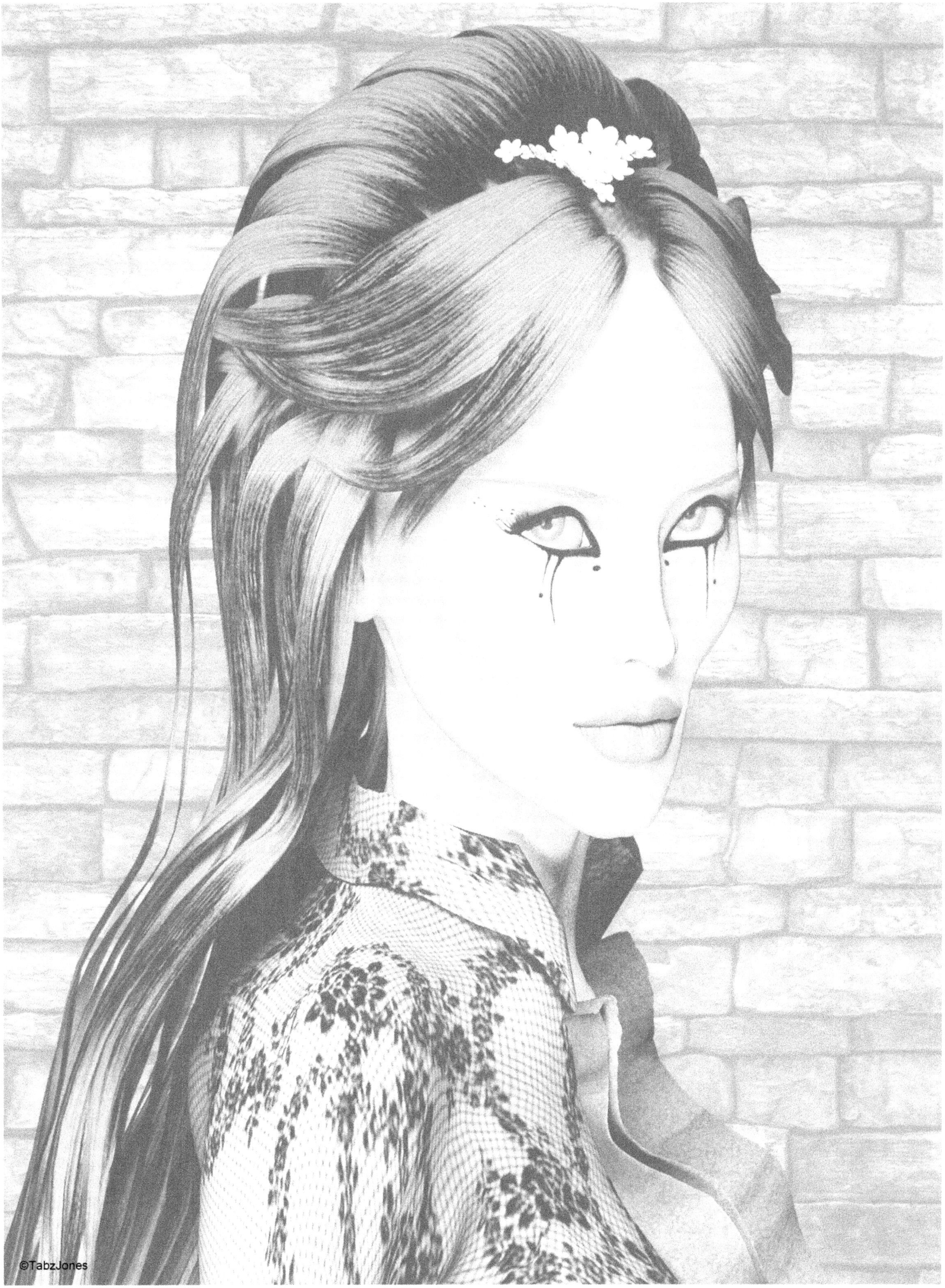

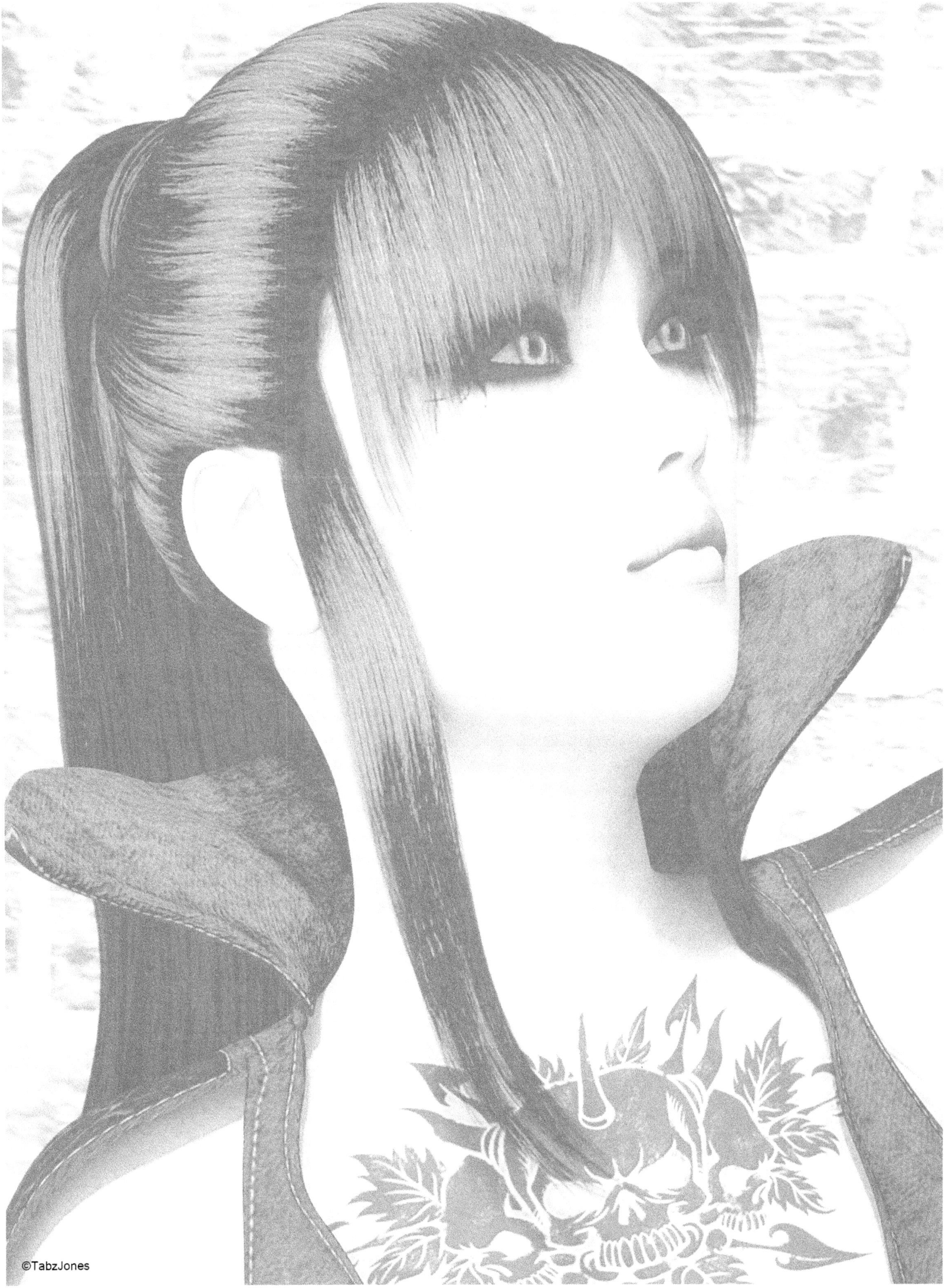

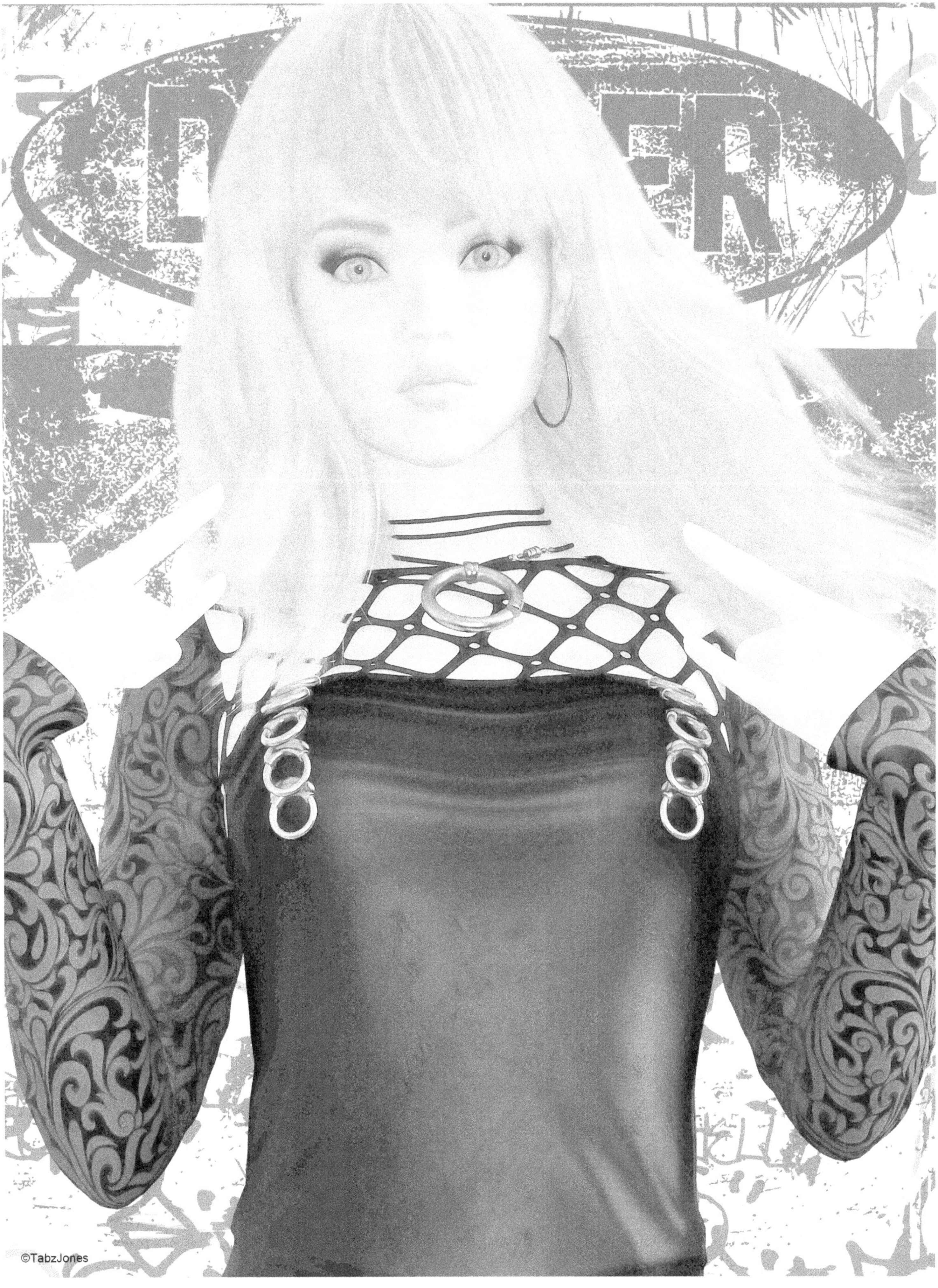

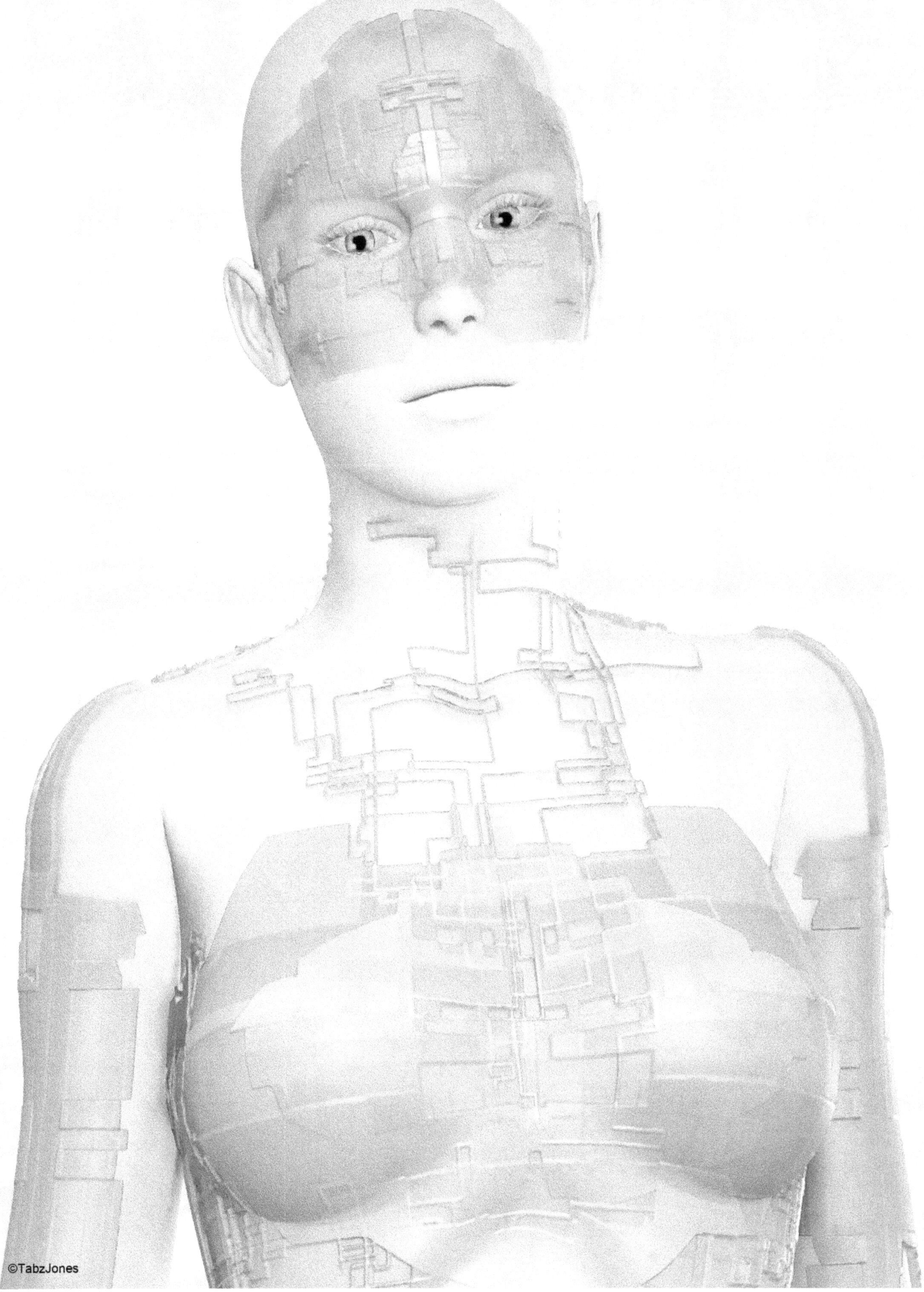

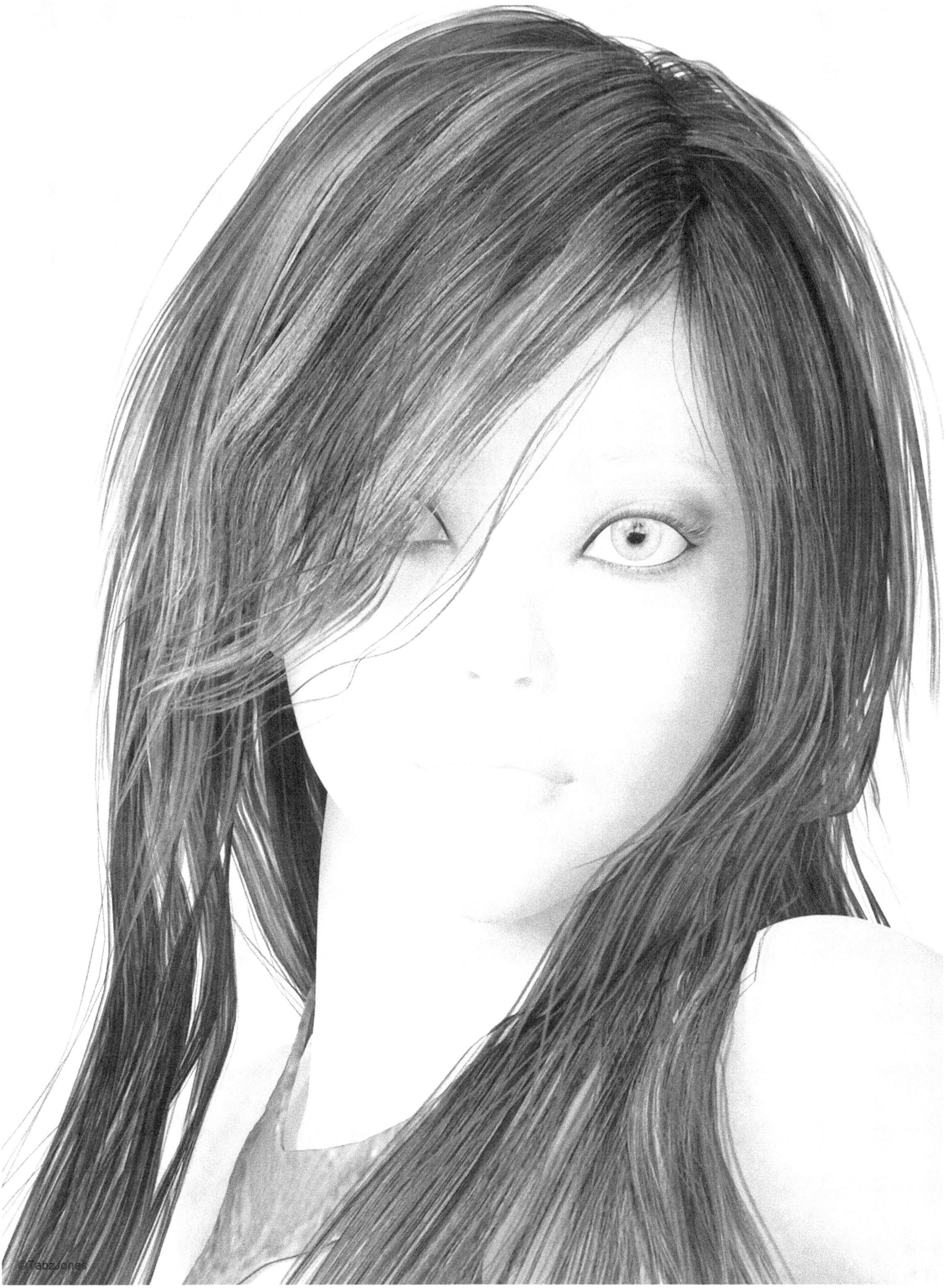
©TabzJones

www.ingramcontent.com/pod-product-compliance
Lightning Source LLC
Chambersburg PA
CBHW080137240526
45468CB00009BA/2511
* 9 7 8 1 7 9 6 6 6 2 2 9 0 *